ANTARCTICA

A TRUE BOOK

by
David Petersen

Children's Press®
A Division of Grolier Publishing
New York London Hong Kong Sydney
Danbury, Connecticut

A baby elephant seal

Reading Consultant
Linda Cornwell
Learning Resource Consultant
Indiana Department of
Education

Visit Children's Press on the Internet at:
http://publishing.grolier.com

Library of Congress Cataloging-in-Publication Data

Petersen, David, 1946–
    Antarctica / by David Petersen.
        p.   cm. — (A True book)
    Includes bibliographical references and index.
    Summary: An overview of the history, geography, climate, and wildlife
of Antarctica.
    ISBN: 0-516-20770-9 (lib. bdg.)   0-516-26426-5 (pbk.)
    1. Antarctica—Juvenile literature. 2. Natural history-
Antarctica—Juvenile literature. [1. Antarctica.] I. Title.
II. Series.
G863.P48 1998
919.8—dc21   98-25106
                                                                                    CIP
                                                                                    AC

Contents

This satellite image of Antarctica, taken from high above the earth, shows that most of the continent is covered by ice.

Antarctica— A Frozen World

Of Earth's seven continents, only one, Antarctica, has no rivers, no forests, and no native people. Very few creatures of any kind can live in the interior of this continent.

This is because Antarctica is the coldest place on Earth,

and it is almost completely covered with ice. In 1983, the world-record low temperature of -128.6 degrees Fahrenheit (-89.2 degrees Celsius) was recorded there.

In the permanently frozen
Antarctic interior, the temperature reaches the freezing
point—which is 32 degrees
Fahrenheit (0 degrees C)—
on only the mildest summer
days. Nearer the sea coasts,
it gets a little warmer, but it
is still bitterly cold most of
the year.

Why is this?

Antarctica, hidden at the
bottom of the globe, is shad-
ed from the sun's most direct

During Antarctica's summer—December through March—the sun never sets.

and warmest light. The sunlight it does receive is so weak that it doesn't warm up the continent very much.

The Antarctic winter—May through August—is brutally cold. For much of the winter, the sun never rises over most

8

of Antarctica. In summer—
December through March—
the sun never sets in these
areas. But the sun is so low in
the sky that most of its heat is
reflected away by the ice.

Antarctica represents almost all of the world's ice surface.

Antarctica is also one of the windiest places on Earth. Near the coasts, gusts of wind often reach speeds of 120 miles (190 kilometers) per hour.

Antarctic Geography

The name Antarctica means "opposite to the Arctic." The Arctic is the region surrounding the North Pole, at the top of the world. Antarctica surrounds the South Pole, at the bottom of the globe.

On a map, you'll find Antarctica below South America.

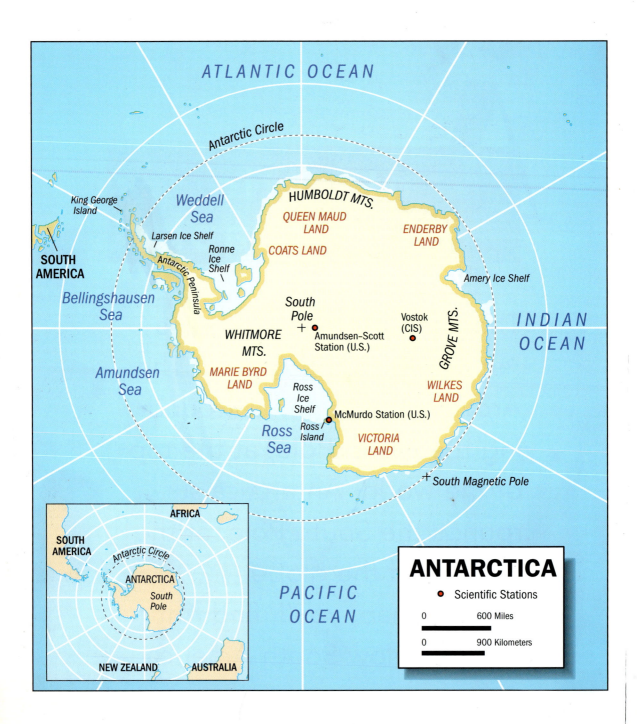

ATLANTIC OCEAN

Antarctic Circle

King George
Island

Weddell
Sea

Larsen Ice Shelf

SOUTH
AMERICA

Antarctic Peninsula

Ronne
Ice
Shelf

HUMBOLDT MTS.

QUEEN MAUD
LAND

COATS LAND

ENDERBY
LAND

Amery Ice Shelf

Bellingshausen
Sea

South
Pole
+

WHITMORE
MTS.

Vostok
(CIS)

GROVE MTS.

INDIAN
OCEAN

Amundsen-Scott
Station (U.S.)

Amundsen
Sea

MARIE BYRD
LAND

Ross
Ice
Shelf

WILKES
LAND

Ross
Sea

Ross
Island

McMurdo Station (U.S.)

VICTORIA
LAND

South Magnetic Pole

AFRICA

SOUTH
AMERICA

Antarctic Circle

ANTARCTICA

South
Pole

NEW ZEALAND   AUSTRALIA

PACIFIC
OCEAN

ANTARCTICA

● Scientific Stations

0   600 Miles

0   900 Kilometers

In fact, the two continents are separated by only 700 miles (1,100 km) of ocean.

Like other continents, Antarctica has mountains, valleys, even lakes. But in most areas, these features are invisible, buried beneath thick ice.

Some mountain peaks do rise above the layer of ice. And in a few places, the ice has disappeared, leaving behind spectacular "dry valleys." High winds keep snow from collecting in the dry valleys.

In some areas of Antarctica, mountain peaks rise above the layers of ice (left). High winds keep snow from collecting, leaving "dry valleys" (below).

In places, the Antarctic ice cap is 15,700 feet (4,800 meters) thick. That's more than ten times the height of one of the world's tallest buildings.

If you're wondering how all that ice got there—it fell as snow, a little at a time, over millions of years. Including its ice cap, Antarctica occupies 5.4 million square miles (14 million square km), making it larger than Australia or Europe. But melt away the ice, and Antarctica becomes Earth's smallest continent.

The ice cap also changes Antarctica's elevation. With the ice, Antarctica averages 7,500 feet (2,300 m) above sea level, becoming Earth's highest continent. Without

The largest glacier discovered in the Antarctic is the Beardmore Glacier, which is about the size of France.

the ice, Antarctica shrinks to only 1,500 feet (460 m) above sea level.

Antarctic Exploration

Antarctica is surrounded by three oceans—the Pacific, the Atlantic, and the Indian.

Cold air blowing off Antarctica freezes the surrounding oceans, forming vast, floating sheets of ice called ice shelves. In summer, the edges of the ice shelves thaw and break apart,

An Antarctic ice shelf (above). In summer, the edges of the ice shelves break apart and fall into the ocean (left).

sending gigantic icebergs sailing out to sea. Some Antarctic icebergs are bigger than the state of Delaware!

An icebreaker ship escorting a cargo ship through the thick ice

Today, visitors to Antarctica arrive by airplane or helicopter. But early explorers had to come by boat. For centuries, icebergs and stormy seas kept cautious sailors from approaching the frozen continent. The first sighting of the Antarctic mainland wasn't made until 1820. Historians aren't sure who the first person was to set foot on Antarctica. Many believe that in 1821 an American whale hunter named John Davis became the first to reach the continent. A group of Norwegian whale hunters definitely landed on Antarctica in 1895.

Soon, hardy adventurers swarmed all over coastal

Antarctica. During the early 1900s, explorers competed to see who would be the first to reach the South Pole. That race was won on December 14,

1911, by Norwegian explorer Roald Amundsen and four companions. Traveling on skis and using dogs to pull their supplies on sleds, Amundsen's party made the trip in less than two months. Better yet, all five men returned safely home to tell their heroic stories to their children.

Another team of explorers wasn't so lucky. British captain Robert Falcon Scott and four companions reached the South Pole on January 17, 1912,

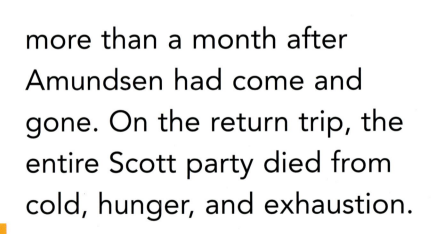

more than a month after Amundsen had come and gone. On the return trip, the entire Scott party died from cold, hunger, and exhaustion.

Antarctic Wildlife

Looking at Antarctica today, it's hard to believe that this was once a warm, gentle land, green with trees and plants. But that is what Antarctica was like about 150 million years ago.

Today, few living things can survive the cold, dry weather

More than four hundred species of mosses have been found on Antarctica and nearby islands.

of this remote continent. Mosses are the most common plants in Antarctica. They grow mostly near the coast.

26

Simple algae and lichens also grow on the continent.

No mammal can live in Antarctica's freezing interior. The only animals that spend their entire lives on the continent are tiny creatures such as fleas, lice, mites, spiders, and other bugs and insects.

But out in the Antarctic seas and along the coast, things are a whole lot livelier. Millions of inch-long, shrimp-like creatures called krill swim

in the waters around the continent. Krill are good to eat, and they provide the food base for many animals, including fish, squid, whales, seals, penguins, and birds.

Antarctic Whales

Whales, like people, are warm-blooded, air-breathing mammals. The blue whale is the largest animal in the world. Today the blue whale is protected from hunters by law. They can grow to be up to 100 feet (30 m) long and weigh as much as 150 tons. Such a whale can eat more than 4 tons of krill per day!

Only five species of hair-seals are found along the Antarctic coast.

Antarctica's most common seals are called crabeaters. But despite their name, crabeaters don't actually eat crabs. They eat krill.

The southern elephant seal gets its name from its floppy

snout, which it can inflate like a balloon. Antarctica's elephant seals can be as long as 21 feet (6.4 m).

The leopard seal, like the killer whale, hunts for a living. Its favorite prey are small seals and penguins.

On land, penguins waddle along on their webbed feet. In the water, a penguin uses its wings like a fish uses its fins. When penguins aren't speeding through the water after fish

Emperor penguins can weigh up to 80 pounds (36 kilograms).

and other seafood, they climb onto the ice to rest, socialize, and raise their young.

The emperor penguin is Antarctica's largest bird. It

stands up to 4 feet (1.2 m) tall. Emperors do not build nests. Instead, after a female lays one giant egg, her mate places it on top of his feet to keep it off the ice. He then warms it with his lower belly until it hatches.

Many other species of sea-birds live in the skies above the penguins, seals, and whales. These birds include petrels, skuas, terns, gulls, and albatrosses. Some of these birds feed on krill, while others eat the eggs of fish and birds.

Albatross (left) and skuas (right) are two birds that live in Antarctica.

Skuas and petrels have been spotted deep in the interior of Antarctica. This leads scientists to believe that these birds may occasionally fly across the continent.

Earth's Grandest Laboratory

Few places on Earth offer as many opportunities for scientific study as Antarctica. Every summer, researchers from all over the world visit Antarctica to study the land, the air, the weather, the wildlife, the water, and the ice.

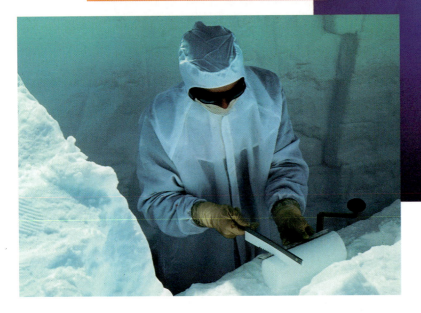

A researcher examines the inside of a glacier crevasse (right). A scientist saws off a piece of an ice core (below).

Other scientists come to study earthquakes, sunlight, and astronomy.

The largest research center on Antarctica is McMurdo Station, maintained by the United States on Ross Island. Every summer, about a thousand scientists and support

The Ross Ice Shelf on McMurdo Sound (left). The American flag waves above the McMurdo Station (below).

staff make McMurdo their temporary home. Fewer than two hundred people stay during the dark, cold winter.

Dozens of other countries maintain scientific stations on Antarctica. Forty-two nations have signed an agreement called the Antarctic Treaty. This agreement states that the continent should only be used for peaceful, scientific purposes. It also sets rules that protect Antarctica's delicate environment.

Many countries maintain scientific stations on Antarctica.

The Antarctic Treaty is the first and most successful agreement of its kind. It is an encouraging example of how nations can work together for peace and knowledge.

Antarctica Today

For thousands of years, nobody knew that Antarctica lay hidden at the bottom of the globe. The first people to set foot on the continent were much like today's astronauts. They were exploring a world never before seen by human beings.

Scientists study satellite images at McMurdo Station, the largest research center on Antarctica.

Today, much of Antarctica has been explored by scientists, but it is still a cold and mysterious continent. Few

Today Antarctica remains a mysterious and fascinating continent.

people get to go to Antarctica. Perhaps someday you will have a chance to visit this frozen, fascinating continent.

Antarctica Fast Facts

Area including ice cap: 5.4 million square miles (14 million sq km)

Greatest thickness of ice cap 15,700 feet (4,800 m)

Average thickness of ice cap 7,100 feet (2,200 m)

Coastline including permanent ice: 19,800 miles (31,900 km)

Highest elevation Vinson Massif: 16,864 feet (5,140 m) above sea level

Average elevation including ice cap: 7,500 feet (2,300 m) above sea level; without ice cap: 1,500 feet (460 m) above sea level

Coldest temperature 128.6 degrees below zero Fahrenheit (-89.2 degrees C), recorded July 21, 1983 at the Soviet Union's Vostok scientific station

To Find Out More

Here are some additional resources to help you learn more about the continent of Antarctica:

 **Books**

Dunn, Margery. **Exploring Your World: The Adventure of Geography.** National Geographic, 1993.

Holmes, Kevin J. **Penguins.** Children's Press, 1997.

Mariner, Tom. **Continents.** Marshall Cavendish, 1990.

Markert, Jenny. **Glaciers & Icebergs.** Child's World, 1993.

Planet Earth: World Geography. Oxford University Press, 1993.

Rosenthal, Paul. **Where on Earth?** Knopf, 1992.

Rotter, Charles. **Seals & Sea Lions.** Child's World, 1991.

Stone, Lynne. **Antarctica: The Land.** Rourke Bk., 1995.

Taylor, Barbara. **Arctic & Antarctic.** Knopf, 1995.

Organizations and Online Sites

**Antarctica:
Weather Watch**
*http://www.compuquill.com/
aohtml/aoww0000.html*

In addition to providing the latest weather forecast in Antarctica, this site offers creative, fun projects for kids of all ages.

Glacier Land
*http://www.glacier.rice.edu/
chapters/land/5_
antarcticesheetfirst.html*

Take a tour of Antarctica as scientists discuss the history and formation of glaciers.

Live from Antarctica
*http://quest.arc.nasa.gov/
antarctica/index.html*

Lots of information about Antarctica. Check out the electronic field trip designed especially for students.

**McMurdo Station:
A Virtual Tour**
*http://astro.uchicago.edu/
cara/vtour/mcmurdo/*

An exciting look at life inside the largest research center on Antarctica.

Office of National Tourism
*http://www.tourism.gov.au/
new/cfa/cfa_fs17.html*

All kinds of information on the continent's geography, climate, early explorations, and the laws protecting Antarctica.

Penguins
*http://www.birminghamzoo.
com/ao/penguins.htm*

Great color photos and information on more than seventeen species of penguins.

Important Words

astronomy the scientific study of planets, stars, and other objects in space

continent one of seven large land masses of the earth

elevation the height to which something is raised

ice cap a large mass of of ice flowing out in several directions from the central mass

ice shelf a great wall of ice

mammal air-breathing, warm-blooded vertebrates in which the female nourish their young with milk; generally covered with body hair.

sea level the level of the surface of the sea

46

Index

Meet the Author

David Petersen is the author of several books on natural history, including *Among the Elk* (Northland Publishing), and *Ghost Grizzlies* (Henry Holt). In the True Book's series for Children's Press, he has written books on every continent and many national parks. David lives in Colorado with his wife, Caroline. He likes to read, write, walk in the woods, camp, hunt, fly fish, and explore the world.

DATE DUE

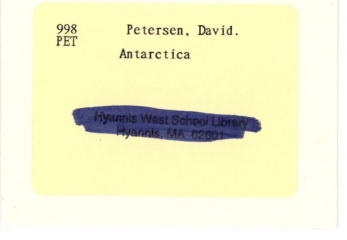